Flip pages here for

THE SPECIAL EFFECTS COOKBOOK

BY
MICHAEL E. SAMONEK

PUBLISHED BY: MES / FX PUBLISHING
P.O. BOX 863, Narberth, PA 19072

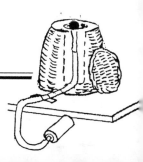

The Special Effects Cookbook can also be used as a coloring book by the young ones!

At the corners of the cookbook, you'll notice little drawings, which are part of animation or "flip" books. When you flip through the pages of the book quickly, you animate the recipes, showing you how they'll perform when you make them!

EARN $50.00 to $100

Send us a videotape or picture of people having fun with one of our Special Effects Cookbook recipes, and if we use it in our next commercial, we'll pay you $50.00! Or send us a videotape or a picture and detailed description of your own original Special Effects Recipe, and if we use it, we'll pay you $100.00!

Send your tapes, pictures and recipes to:

SFX RECIPE SUBMISSIONS
P.O. BOX 863
NARBERTH, PA 19072

COPYRIGHT © 1992 BY MICHAEL E. SAMONEK

ISBN 0-9632877-0-2

Library of Congress Catalog Card Number 92-90755

ALL ILLUSTRATIONS BY
FINNIN STUDIOS

PRINTED IN U.S.A.

PLEASE PLAY IT SAFE!
The Author and Publisher urge that children should be supervised by adults in all cooking situations. Care should be taken when using the stove or oven, knives, dry ice, pots and pans, and other kitchen tools and ingredients. We want you to realize that while the kitchen is a fun place, it can also be a dangerous place. Many different things can hurt you if you are not careful. That is why it is important to have adult supervision.

FOREWORD

It is difficult to say what can spark an imaginative and inquisitive mind. Many inventors and scientists credit a museum experience or a particular teacher or mentor. The richness of experience in the home is also a keen stimulus.

Michael E. Samonek offers us a new vehicle to enrich the home environment and to foster a sense of wonder and excitement. He suggests that you can make it, or bake it using materials you can find in your own home. This is indeed a creative thought.

You will have fun trying Samonek's recipes for fun. You will probably invent some of your own. That's great. But better yet, work on these projects with your children and let them explore new ways to make special effects. With this book, there is magic to be done in the kitchen. Call the children and get started.

Ed Sobey, Ph.D.
Executive Director
National Inventors Hall of Fame and
National Invention Center
Akron, Ohio

TABLE OF CONTENTS

FROM THE AUTHOR

I have been asked more than once, "What inspired you to write a book like this?" My reply is as follows:

On a Saturday evening in 1990 I was sitting in the Grand Ballroom of the Disneyland Hotel in Anaheim, California, waiting to receive an award for a device I invented: the VideotapeMeasure™, a device for measuring the amount of tape time remaining on a videocassette. It had won first place in the tools catagory in the Second Annual Great Idea Contest sponsored by the Inventors Workshop International Education Foundation.

The keynote speaker that evening was Dr. Edwin J.C. Sobey, executive director of the National Inventor's Hall of Fame. In his speech, titled, "Who Will Invent The 21st Century?", he spoke of how American students are falling behind their peers around the world in science and mathematics. He said that by the eighth grade, 80% of American students are science drop-outs- mainly because they have been convinced science is NOT FUN!

It came to me that the persuasion that science CAN BE FUN should begin at a very early age – when children are playing. When playing they like the things that are unusual, things that move, that make noise, that glitter and glow. And they like animals – the more exotic the better. Combine that with food and imagination and you have invention. And science has crept in painlessly and is FUN.

Hence this cookbook. If it encourages children to express themselves creatively, if it inspires them to pursue a career in science later and a new and better 21st century is invented – it will have served its purpose.

Michael E. Samonek
July 21st, 1991

Section One
Special Visual
Effects

Recipe Notes:

Erupting Volcano Cake

EIGHT INCH ROUND CAKES STACKED TO FORM A VOLCANO SHAPE THAT ACTUALLY ERUPTS DELICIOUS RED FOAM "LAVA" AND HUGE CLOUDS OF MYSTERIOUS, SAFE, ODOR-FREE, DISAPPEARING "SMOKE"!

For this special effect you will need;

- Six 8" baked round cakes (your favorite).
- Brown and Green frosting.
- One fresh egg with shell scrubbed clean.
- One small juice glass or 1 and a half inch cookie cutter.
- 2-3 drops red food coloring.
- One and a half teaspoons sugar.
- One quarter pound dry ice.
- Aluminum foil.
- One to two ounces hot tap water.

Make six eight inch round cakes using your favorite mix or buy the cakes from a bakery.

Buy two or three dollars worth of Dry Ice from an ice cream store the day you will need it. Keep the dry ice in the freezer. Be sure to handle the dry ice with gloves or tongs just to be safe. If your ice cream store doesn't have dry ice just look in your local Yellow Pages telephone directory under DRY ICE. It's easy to find everywhere.

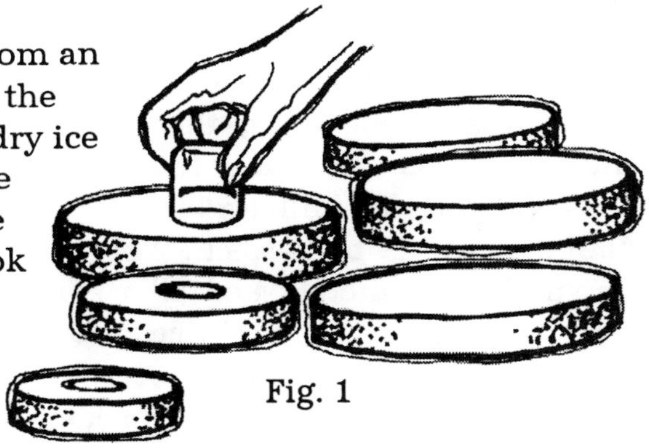

Fig. 1

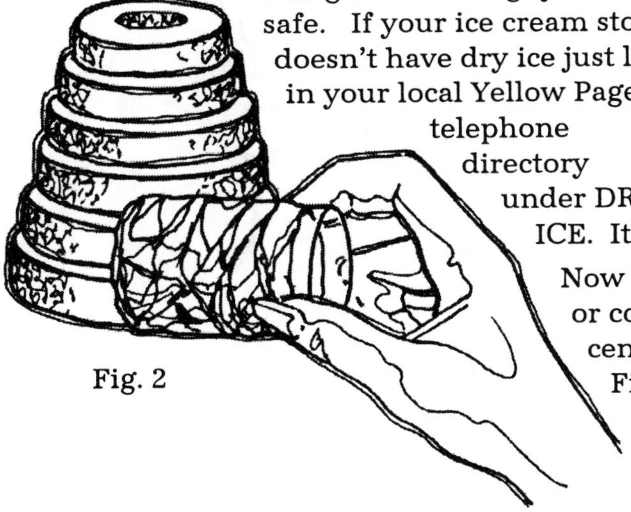

Fig. 2

Now use your juice glass or cookie cutter and cut out a hole in the center of the top two layers of cake. See Fig. 1. This hole will form a well in the center of the cake and hide the special effect.

Now construct the Volcano Cake, round pyramid style, on a cake platter or large dish. Trim each layer into successively smaller rounds and stack and frost them into a mountain shape using the last two layers with the holes as it's top.

With a small piece of aluminum foil, line the well in the center of the volcano cake. Use the juice glass as a mold and form the foil around the glass. See Fig. 2.

Now frost the cake, smoothing out the small step-like ledges. Use chocolate frosting for the whole cake first. Then use green frosting as highlights around the mountain to resemble vegetation.

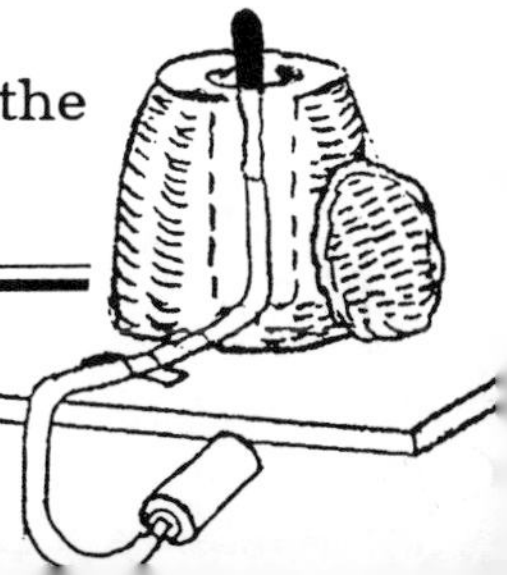

When you are ready to serve the cake, make the "lava". Separate the cleaned egg and discard the yolk. Put the egg white in a small mixing bowl with one and one half teaspoons sugar and two or three drops of red food coloring. Beat until the egg white starts to thicken. You don't want stiff peaks to form, just a thick, foamy texture.

Now place two or three small chunks of dry ice into the foil-lined well of the cake and pour in the red egg mixture. Nothing much will happen yet. Now fill your juice glass with hot tap water and take the Volcano Cake and water to the table where your guests are. When you are ready to produce the Special Effect, simply pour one or two ounces of the hot water into the egg and dry ice mixture and your realistic Volcano Cake will erupt large quantities of orange, foamy "lava" and white "smoke" for several minutes while you serve your delighted guests pieces of genuine Erupting Volcano Cake!

ALTERNATE FOAM GENERATING TECHNIQUE FOR "ERUPTING VOLCANO CAKE

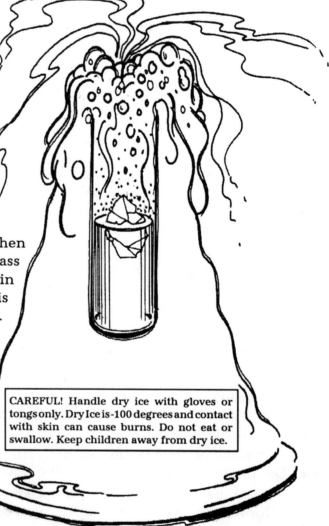

If you cannot find dry ice in your area, you can still produce the foaming "Lava" effect. There will be no smoke, but you will have plenty of foamy "Lava"! You will need a small, short juice glass or shot glass that will fit snugly in the center hole of the Volcano Cake (a glass 3" tall and 1-1/2" in diameter would be perfect). You will also need one small box of Jell-o®, one small bottle of lemon juice and 1 tablespoon of bicarbonate of soda. Make the Jell-o® according to package directions. Let cool for 15 minutes. When Jell-o® is still warm (not hot), fill juice glass 1/2 full with the warm Jell-o®. Pour in enough lemon juice so that the glass is almost full, or about 1/2" from the top. Place the glass down into the hole in the cake so lip of glass is flush with the top of the cake. You are now ready to produce the special effect. When ready, put one tablespoon of bicarbonate of soda into the glass and briefly stir (1-2 seconds). Jell-o® foam will immediately pour out of the top of the glass and flow down the sides of the Volcano Cake.

CAREFUL! Handle dry ice with gloves or tongs only. Dry Ice is -100 degrees and contact with skin can cause burns. Do not eat or swallow. Keep children away from dry ice.

Jell-o® is a registered trademark of General Foods.

ALTERNATE METHOD FOR MAKING "ERUPTING VOLCANO CAKE"

Instead of stacking successively smaller cake rounds to form a conical pyramid, just buy 2 angel food cakes. Slice off the top 3" of one and place it on the other to form the volcano cake. Cut off the square edge of the top layer to achieve the round mountain effect.

Stuff wadded-up paper into lower cake hole to support juice glass and special effect, which will accommodate either the dry ice method, or the gelatin, lemon juice and sodium bicarbonate method explained in the alternate foam recipe.

Erupting Volcano Cake!

Green Dragon's Breath Cake

A SHEET CAKE IN THE SHAPE OF A DRAGON WHICH ACTUALLY BREATHES OUT HUGE CLOUDS OF MYSTERIOUS, SAFE, ODORFREE, DISAPPEARING "SMOKE"!

For this Special Effect you will need:
- One 13" X 9" sheet Cake-Your favorite flavor
- Two sheets tracing Paper, 8½" X 11" and a pencil
- Tape and scissors
- 15" X 11" foil lined cardboard base
- 5" high coat box at least 13" X 9"
- Plastic 3" or 4" round deli container with tight fitting lid
- Plastic drinking straw
- Green frosting
- Red frosting in a squeeze tube from the store
- 1/4 lb. dry ice

Make your favorite 13" by 9" sheet cake or buy one from a bakery. Place sheet cake on foil-lined cardboard base.

Tape together two 8½" by 11" sheets of tracing paper to make one 17" by 11" sheet. Trace the dragon pattern on pages 14 & 15. Cut out the dragon shape pattern. Place dragon pattern on cake and cut around pattern with a knife to form the dragon shape cake. Save cake cuttings and brush away crumbs.

Frost cake with green frosting. Use premixed red frosting in a squeeze tube from the store and form the eye, nostril and scale patterns to resemble a real dragon character. See illustrations.

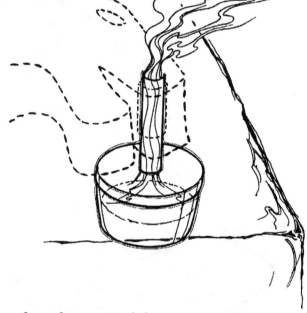

Now take the 5" high coat box and cut away and remove one whole long, narrow side so you can reach into the empty box from that side with ease. Place the frosted cake on top of this box.

Take a sharp skewer and poke a hole through the dragon's nostril down all the way through the cardboard base and coat box. Ream the hole out so that the plastic straw will fit snugly. Now insert the straw down through the nostril all the way into the coat box so it cannot be seen on the surface of the cake.

Now poke a hole in the center of the plastic deli container lid just so the plastic straw will fit snugly. Reach into the box with the lid and fit the lid onto the straw so that about 1" of the straw sticks into the underside of the lid. See illustration above. You are now ready to produce the Special effect.

When you are ready to present the Breathing Dragon Special Effect, place three or four walnut sized chunks of dry ice into the empty deli container and half fill it with hot tap water. (Large amounts of CO_2 vapor will immediately pour out. Don't be afraid of this. It is quite harmless). Now quickly place the smoking deli container inside the box and fit

the lid/straw tightly over the container. The vapor, now under pressure, will shoot up through the straw and out the dragon's nostril!

The dragon cake will breath out this safe, harmless, disappearing "smoke" for several minutes while the kids jump up and down with excitement. Everyone who sees this Special Effect LOVES it!

ALTERNATE SMOKE GENERATING EFFECT FOR "GREEN DRAGON'S BREATH CAKE"

If you cannot find dry ice in your area, there are two alternate methods of producing the smoke effect. One is to tape or tie a balloon to one end of a 2 foot piece of 1/4" plastic hose (use the same hose and balloon as used in the "Great Earthquake Cake"). Push the open end of the hose up through the coat box and up through the dragon's nostril. If you blow into the hose, the balloon will inflate. If you blow cigarette or cigar smoke into the balloon, it will inflate with smoke! Blow several mouthfuls of smoke into the balloon, making sure to pinch or crimp the hose shut after every inflation. Do not inhale smoke into your lungs! Once the balloon is 10" to 12" in diameter, clamp the hose shut with a clothespin near the balloon end. Pull the hose back inside the nostril so it can't be seen. Now you are ready to release the clothespin, and the balloon will deflate, pushing the smoke out through the Dragon's nostril. (Note: Don't wait more than a minute or 2 to deflate the balloon, or the smoke will settle inside the balloon and ruin the effect.) WARNING: DO NOT INHALE TOBACCO SMOKE. The Surgeon General warns that inhaling tobacco smoke may be injurious to your health.

The other alternate smoke effect is easy. Just line the nostril with aluminum foil and place a piece of lighted, cone incense into the nostril. It will smoke for several minutes and add a nice aroma to your party room.

CAREFUL! Handle dry ice with gloves or tongs only. Dry Ice is -100 degrees and contact with skin can cause burns. Do not eat or swallow. Keep children away from dry ice.

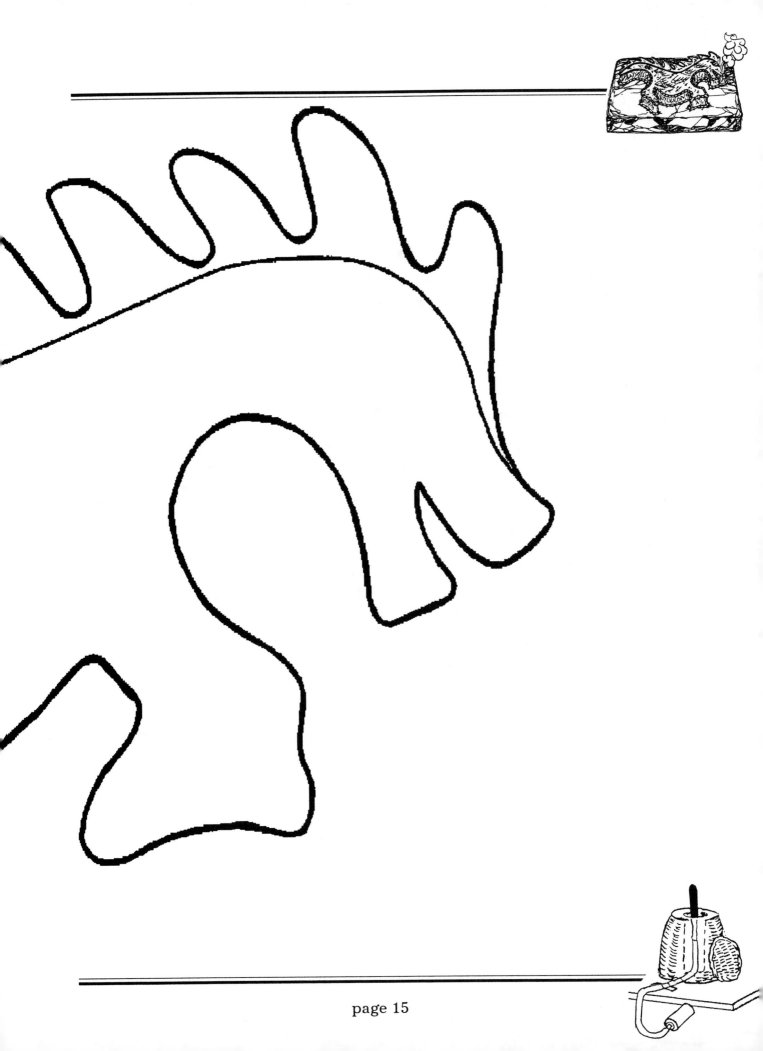

Glow in the Dark Gelatin

"A JELLO MOLD THAT LIGHTS UP AND GLOWS EERILY WHEN YOU TURN OUT THE LIGHTS"!

For this Special Effect you will need:

- Your favorite flavor gelatin (red or green Looks best!)
- Mold pan
- Bundt cake pan or angel food cake pan
- Transparent glass plate
- Small flashlight

Make your favorite flavor of gelatin and pour into a mold or just use a suitable bowl.

The secret to this special effect is the base on which you will display the gelatin mold.

Fig. 1

Take a bundt cake pan or an angel food cake pan with a hollow cylinder center where you can insert a small flashlight. Unmold the gelatin onto a clear, transparent glass plate which will allow the light to pass through and illuminate the gelatin. Place the plate on the cake pan display stand with the lit flashlight in the central cylinder pointing up. See Fig. 1. Now turn out the lights and present an eerie, glowing gelatin mold that will delight any child.

You may want to line the outside of the cake pan with cardboard you have painted with a glow in the dark paint. This really enhances the effect.

If you don't have a bundt or angel food cake pan, just make a stand from a strip of corrugated card-board rolled into an eight inch round to accommodate your flashlight and hold your clear glass cake plate.

Self Decorating Cake

"A CAKE THAT ACTUALLY DECORATES ITSELF WITH A CASCADE OF COLORFUL CAKE SPRINKLES AS GUESTS WATCH IN AMAZEMENT"!

For this Special effect You will need:

- Two 8" cake rounds
- White frosting
- Three colored round balloons
- One Helium filled balloon from balloon store
- One sparkler
- Thin ribbon
- Cake decorating Sprinkles
- Wire Cake Rack

Place the two 8" cake rounds side by side on a wire rack and frost with white frosting. Don't stack the cake layers. The side by side arrangement allows more surface area for the cake sprinkles to fall.

Take three colored round balloons and pour into each one a small quantity of multi-colored cake sprinkles, small candies, etc. Don't fill the balloons! Just put enough in each balloon so it will still float without giving away the secret to the special effect. Blow up the balloons and tie them off.

Go to a balloon store and have them fill a fourth, larger balloon with Helium Gas. This balloon will hold up or suspend the other three loaded "balloon bombs" over the bare cakes. Tie this suspension balloon to a center wire between the two cakes on the wire rack, so it hovers directly over the two cakes.

Now tie the three "balloon bombs" below the large suspension balloon in a cluster so they each touch one another. Next tie the sparkler slightly below the balloon cluster so that the sparkler will eventually burn up to the balloon cluster and pop them with it's heat.

When you are ready for the Special effect, tell everyone to stand back and watch as you light the sparkler. This looks festive enough, but the real special effect occurs when the sparkler touches the balloon cluster, bursting a shower of cake sprinkles down and over the two cakes, decorating itself!

"Fire Eyes" Skeleton Cake

"A GHOSTLY HALLOWEEN CAKE IN THE SHAPE OF A SKELETON WITH EYES THAT ARE ACTUALLY ON FIRE"!

For this Special Effect you will need:

- One 13" X 9" sheet cake- your favorite flavor
- Aluminum Foil
- 15" X 30" sheet of heavy cardboard
- Chocolate frosting
- White frosting
- Two sugar cubes
- Lemon extract
- Matches

Bake your favorite rectangular cake in a nine inch by 13 inch pan.- Cool and cut cake into sections as shown in Fig. 1. Do not use shaded portions of cake. Cover a 15" by 30" piece of heavy cardboard with foil and assemble skeleton cake as shown in Fig. 2.

Frost completely with dark chocolate frosting and let cake sit until frosting forms a skin or light crust. Then frost with white frosting, forming the bones of the skeleton as

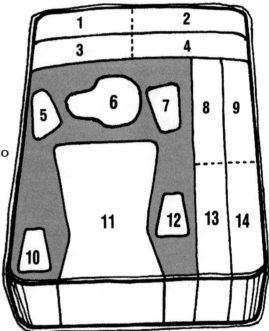

Fig. 1

shown in Fig. 3.

When you are ready to serve this cake place a sugar cube in each eye socket and saturate with lemon extract (peppermint or any other alcohol based flavor extract can also be used).

Now light the sugar cubes with a lit match, turn out the lights and make a very scary entrance at your next Halloween party! See Fig. 4.

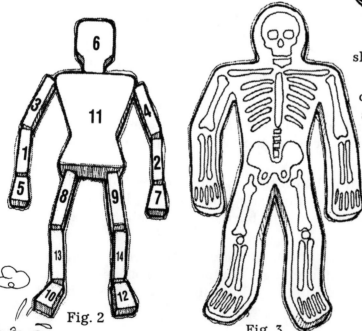

Fig. 2

Fig. 3

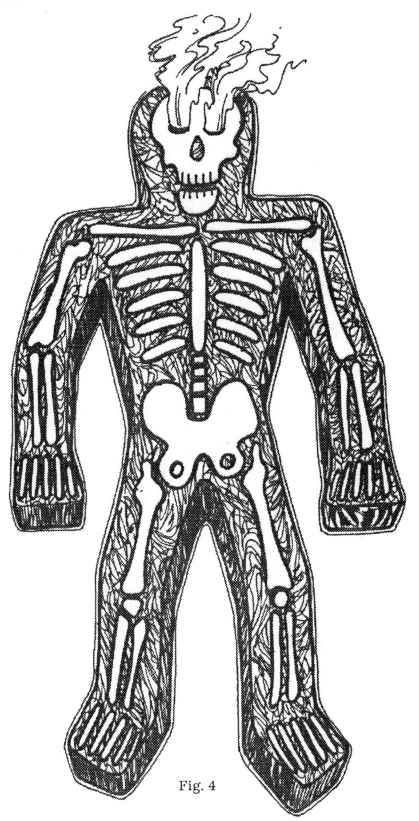

Fig. 4

Magic Color Changing Drinks

"MAGICAL FUN WITH YOUR OWN RAINBOW COLOR-CHANGING JUICE BAR"!

Pour a glass three-quarters full of purple grape juice. Use unsweetened, natural grape juice with no additives.

Now add a small amount of freshly squeezed lemon juice and the purple grape juice instantly becomes red grape juice!

Now add one sodium bicarbonate tablet or better still, add the fizzing vitamin tablet described in the Mobile Special Effects section of this book, and the red grape juice will gradually change back to the original purple color and then on to blue! Set up a magic "Rainbow Juice Bar" at your child's next birthday party and watch the wonder on their faces as the juice magically changes color.

For even more fun with magic color changing drinks, try the following;
You will need:
One red cabbage
Knife
Saucepan
Sieve
Ice-tray and 3 glasses

Chop the cabbage and put in saucepan. Cover cabbage with water and bring to a boil. Let cool. Pour cooled cabbage juice and cabbage into sieve held over the sauce pan. Discard cabbage. Pour cooled cabbage juice into ice tray and freeze.

Now you are ready for the magic. Take three glasses and fill one half-full with lemonade or a mixture of lemon juice and water. Fill the second glass half full with plain water and add one, sodium bicarbonate tablet. Fill the third glass half full with plain water. When you are ready for the special effect, drop two or three cabbage juice ice cubes into each glass and watch as the lemonade turns pink, the soda water turns green and the plain water turns purple!

Edible Folded Paper

"HOW TO MAKE FANTASTIC EDIBLE FOLDED PAPER CREATIONS TO DECORATE WITH, THEN EAT"!

For this Special Effect you will need:

- Large sheet of Rice Paper
- Two damp towels
- Exacto knife or razor blade knife
- Peanut oil for frying
- Skillet
- Book on paper folding (Optional)

You can buy large sheets of rice paper from an Oriental food store and make amazing, edible, folded paper creations! Here is a simple recipe for a three dimensional star you can use to dress up a dinner table or decorate a Christmas tree.

The rice paper comes in large sheets, so first cut the sheet to the desired size. Make the star as big as you want, but remember it must fit in a frying pan.

Now put the sheet of paper you cut between two damp towels for about 90 seconds. You want the rice paper to soften up just a little so it becomes workable and holds it's shape. If you soak the paper too long it will become rubbery and will not hold it's shape. Check the paper every 15 seconds to make sure. If necessary, you can use toothpicks or thread to hold the shape you fold until you cook it.

Now take your sheet of paper and draw a five pointed star, then cut the star out. Now with a scoring razor blade knife, score with light pressure lines from each star point to the common meeting place in the center. See Fig. 1. Don't cut all the way through! Turn the star over and score five lines from the crotch to the center. See Fig. 2.

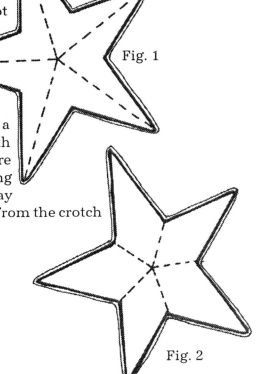

Fig. 1

Fig. 2

Now using both hands, fold the long score lines up and fold the short score line down. After you have your star finished fry it in hot peanut oil until it is golden, which only takes a minute. Dust it with a little powdered sugar and let it cool. I recommend you go to the library and get a book on paper folding. You can make some truly fantastic edible paper creations!

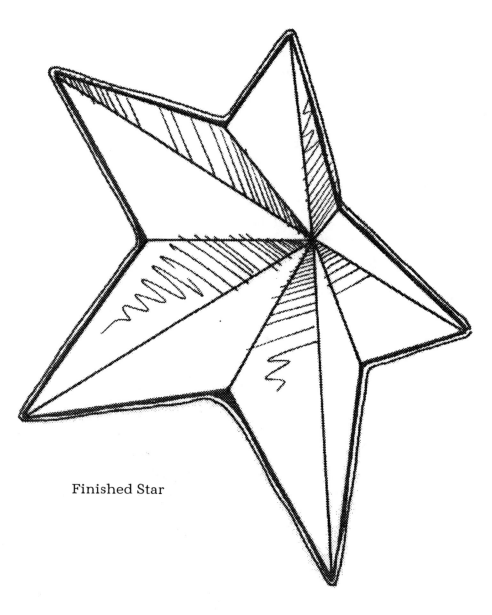

Finished Star

How to Write Under the Shell of an Egg

"HOW TO WRITE A SECRET MESSAGE UNDER THE SHELL OF A HARD-BOILED EGG"!

For this Special Effect you will need:

- Eggs
- Saucepan
- Pencil
- Small needle file
- Food coloring
- Toothpick or tiny brush
- Plaster of Paris and water
- Colored crayons or felt-tipped pens

Easter morning surprises are guaranteed with this simple special effects recipe. First, Hard boil some eggs. For guaranteed perfect hard boiled eggs place eggs in a saucepan and cover with water. Bring to a boil, cover and turn off heat. Let the eggs sit for 20 minutes then pour off the hot water and cover the eggs with cold water until eggs are cool.

Now take a boiled egg and with a pencil, write in block letters a secret message you wish to be revealed on the white of the egg when it is peeled, like "Happy Easter".

With a small needle file, file away the egg shell grooving in your penciled message across the egg. File all the way through the shell so you expose the tender egg white. Once you have your secret message grooved in it's time to color the message.

Dip a toothpick in red food coloring and trace the secret message in the grooves and let dry.

Mix a little plaster of paris and fill in the grooves you just colored. Let dry. Sand away the excess plaster with fine sandpaper carefully. Your plaster patch should now be invisible.

Decorate the egg with colored pencils or crayons.

Don't dip egg in colored water.

Three Color Celery

"HOW TO CREATE A COLORFUL ADDITION TO A DRAB GREEN SALAD"!

For this Special Effect you will need:

- Whole large rib of celery with leaves
- Razor blade knife
- Three glasses of same size
- Three different colors of food coloring
- Water

Take a whole rib of celery <u>with leaves</u>. You must have the leaves intact to make this effect work.

Hold the rib of celery under water in the kitchen sink and cut one inch off the wide end with a razor blade or very sharp knife. Now make two four to five inch slices up from the bottom or wide end of the rib, separating the lower four or five inches of the rib into three separate "legs".

Fill three glasses of the same height with water and into each glass add a few drops of a different color of food coloring, like red, blue and yellow. Group the glasses together and place each "leg" of the celery into a different color-glass.

Refrigerate for several hours or overnight. The colored liquid will have moved up the capillaries in the celery rib, each color separate and distinct. Garnish a salad with a whole rib or just serve a whole plate of three colored celery to brighten up your table. It's guaranteed to cause comment.

Teenage Turtle "Pizza Face" Pizza

TEENAGE TURTLE FANS ARE LEGION AND ARE FED IN TRUE MUTANT FASHION WITH THIS SPECIAL PIZZA. THEY'LL BE SAYING "COWABUNGA!"

For this Special Effect you will need:

- Pizza dough or frozen crust
- Pizza sauce
- Mozzarella cheese
- Two green peppers- minced fine
- Whole pepperoni sausage (not sliced, or strips of Zucchini for vegetarian pizza)
- Black olive

Make your favorite pizza dough recipe or buy frozen pizza dough. Follow package directions to make the crust. When you have formed your round crust spread pizza sauce over the dough and top with mozzarella cheese. To make the turtle face mince two green peppers fine. Sprinkle green minced pepper over the cheese carefully forming a face. See illustration. Cut a whole pepperoni sausage lengthwise into a strip for the mask. From this strip, cut out holes for eyes and place the pepperoni strip on face. Cut a black olive in half for the eyes. Mound a bit more green pepper over the mask for the nose. Cut a long julienne strip of pepperoni for the smiling mouth (*parboil pepperoni first to allow for shrinkage*).

Bake the pizza according to package directions and serve to a gleeful group of Teenage Turtle fans.

Teddy Bear Sandwiches

"BAKE YOUR OWN FRESH TEDDY BEAR SHAPED SANDWICH BREAD FOR THAT WARM, TOASTY FEELING ONLY TEDDY BEARS CAN GIVE"!

For this Special Effect you will need:

- Frozen bread dough
- Cookie sheet
- Egg Wash (beaten egg)
- Sandwich Fillings

The popularity of Teddy Bears guarantees these sandwiches to be a big hit with your kids, and with frozen bread dough, they are easy to make.

Buy frozen bread dough and follow package directions for baking. To form the teddy bears make a large oval about four inches long for the body and a ball for the head. See Fig. 1. Next, make smaller balls of dough for the ears, nose, arms and legs. See Fig. 2.

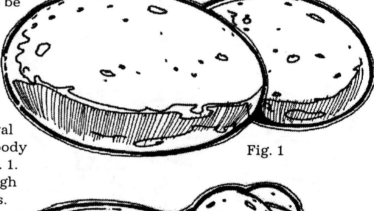

Fig. 1

Place on cookie sheet and brush each teddy bear with egg wash so the bears will come out shiny and golden. Bake according to package directions.

Fig. 2

When you are ready to serve the sandwiches, cut the bears in half and serve with a platter of sandwich fillings so the child can make his own custom made teddy bear sandwich. See Fig. 3.

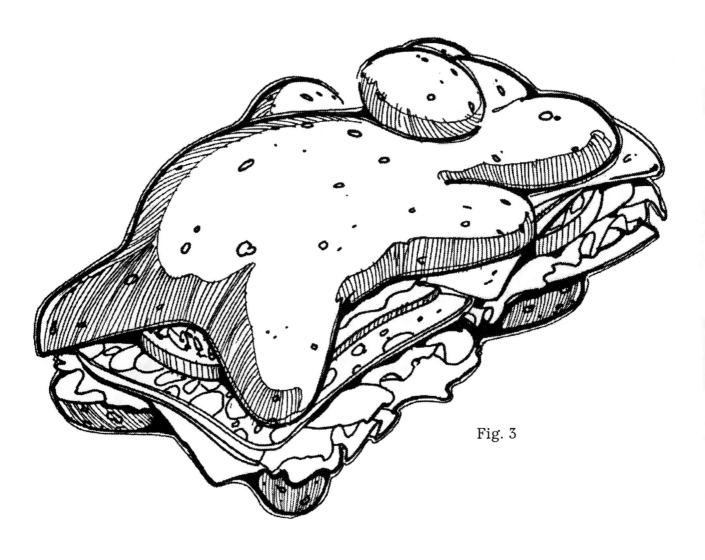

Fig. 3

See-Through Sandwiches

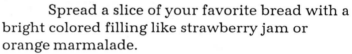

"NO - THEY'RE NOT INVISIBLE, BUT KIDS LOVE THE COLORFUL CUT-OUT DESIGNS THAT MAKE ORDINARY SANDWICHES FUN"!

For this Special Effect you will need:

- Several slices bread
- Jam, jelly, peanut butter, etc.
- Paring knife
- Cookie cutters

Spread a slice of your favorite bread with a bright colored filling like strawberry jam or orange marmalade.

Take the other slice of bread and cut a design right through the bread, like you were carving a Jack-O-Lantern for Halloween.

Now place the cut out slice of bread on the filled slice and you have fun see-through sandwiches.

You can use small cookie cutters to cut out the designs to match the theme of various holidays.

Carrot Caterpillars

"SQUIGGLY VEGETABLES MAKE GOOD NUTRITION FUN"!

For this Special Effect you will need:

- Carrots, zucchini, cucumber, etc.
- Large sewing needle
- Invisible thread
- Large radishes
- Whole cloves

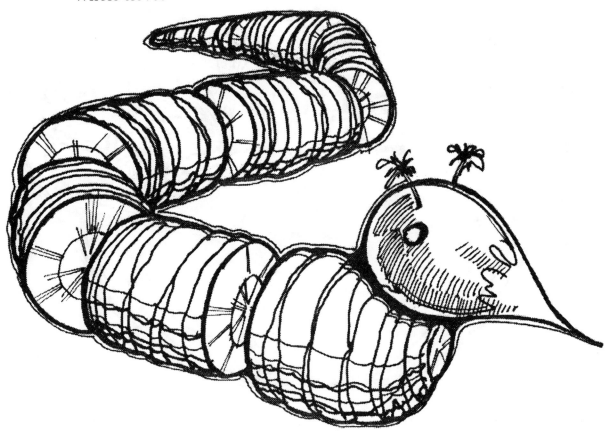

This is a great way to get children to eat fresh, raw vegetables.

Cut a long carrot (you can use zucchini squash, cucumber or any elongated fruit or vegetable) into one inch sections. With a large needle and invisible thread sew together the sections, leaving about one quarter inch between sections. Take a nice long radish and cut out the eye. Attach the radish to the large end with half a toothpick. Stick two whole cloves into the radish for antennae.

Make several out of different vegetables or fruit and watch them disappear at the next kiddie party.

Crocodile in the Salad

"SHARE A SALAD WITH A FRIENDLY CUCUMBER CROCODILE"!

For this Special Effect you will need:

- Gourmet, seedless cucumber
- Black olive
- Tossed green salad
- Radish or slice of tomato

Wash a seedless, gourmet cucumber because you are not going to peel it. Cut off one end to the length of two inches. This piece will stand on the cut end and serve as the crocodile's head. Slice a black Olive and attach two slices for the croc's eyes.

Slice the remaining cucumber in half lengthwise into two equal sections. These are the croc's jaws. Carve "V" shaped teeth into both flat surfaces to resemble teeth.

Now assemble crocodile on top of a tossed, green salad so it looks like the croc is rising up from the depths of the salad bowl. Place a radish or a slice of tomato between the jaws to hold them open and it will look like the crocodile is eating his lunch too!

Brontosaurus Bowl for Dip

"YOU'LL HAVE NO TROUBLE GETTING KIDS TO EAT THEIR VEGETABLES WHEN THEY CAN DO THE "DINOSAUR DIP" WITH THIS CLEVER BIT OF FOOD CARVING"!

For this Special Effect you will need:

- Small acorn squash
- Two Long zucchini squash
- Four small dill pickles
- Toothpicks or bamboo skewers

Cut the top third off the acorn squash, lengthwise. See illustration. Scoop out seeds and pulp. Take one

zucchini and cut a "V" shaped notch about three inches down from the small end, making sure not to cut all the way through. Just cut till you come to the skin. This will form a hinge so the head of the brontosaurus will drop down and rest on the bottom half of the notch. Slice the other end off so you can pin it to the acorn squash with toothpicks. Now cut a small notch for the mouth and insert cloves for the eyes. Attach the other zucchini for the tail. Pin the four dill pickles on for legs.

Fill the dinosaur with your favorite dip and serve as part of the "Dinosaur Diorama" at the end of this book.

Stegasaurus Salad

"TRANSFORM ORDINARY VEGETABLE S INTO A DINOSAUR-SHAPED SALAD"!

For this special effect you will need:

- A large, ripe avocado
- French endive
- Lemon juice
- Lettuce leaves
- A black olive.

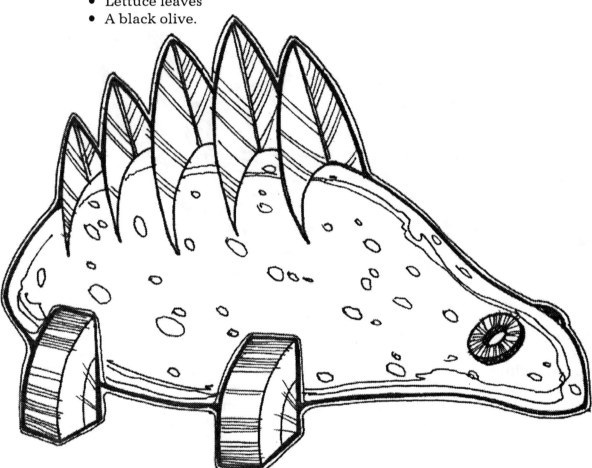

Peel the avocado and slice the bottom fourth off lengthwise so the avocado will sit flat. Sprinkle with lemon juice to prevent discoloration.

Separate endive leaves and choose six or seven, each one a little bigger than the next. Make slits on the top of the avocado and insert the endive leaves to resemble the armor plating of a real stegasaurus. Cut zucchini pieces to resemble legs and put in place. Use black olive slices for eyes.

Assemble stegasaurus on a bed of lettuce, pour on your favorite dressing and serve as part of the "Dinosaur Diorama".

Prehistoric Trees

PLACE THESE VEGETABLE TREES NEXT TO THE STEGASAURAUS SALAD AND WATCH YOUR KIDS TURN INTO HUNGRY "BEAVERS"!

For this Special Effect you will need:

- Large, fat carrot
- Large well formed green pepper
- Paring knife
- Ice Water

Wash a large fat carrot well, but do not peel. Place the carrot upright, large end down, and with a paring knife make downward cuts about an eighth of an inch thick and one inch down, all around the carrot. Move up an inch or so and continue until you have reached the end of the root tip. See illustration. Soak the carrot in ice water and the scales will separate.

Take a green pepper and cut it to resemble a jagged umbrella. This will be the top of the prehistoric tree. See illustration.

Now cut a small hole in the top of the green pepper and place on the tip of the carrot. Use your "Prehistoric Tree" to garnish the "Dinosaur Diorama".

Dinosaur Diorama

AN EDIBLE DINOSAUR "THEME PARTY" THAT LOOKS LIKE THE SET OF A MOVIE"

We all know how popular dinosaurs are with children. Here's how to make the topic of "dinosaurs" the theme of your next children's party. A splendid time is guaranteed for all!

Make your lunch table a "Dinosaur Diorama" by using several of the special effects recipes in this book.

Place the Erupting Volcano Cake in one corner of the table. Place a large punch bowl with the cucumber shark swimming around in circles beside it. Surround Teddy Bear Sandwiches with Prehistoric Trees, Stegasaurus Salads, Brontosaurus Bowls with dip, a Bubbling Witches Cauldron Soup Bowl and you won't have to worry about the entertainment!

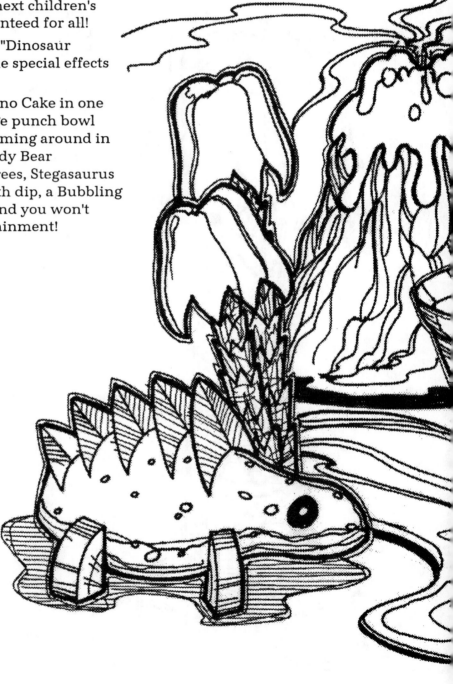

Name Game Herb Garden

"HOW TO MAKE YOUR FAVORITE HERBS GROW IN A SCRIPT PATTERN"

For this recipe you will need:

        1 aluminum sheet cake pan, 13" x 9" x 2"
        1 - 5 lb. bag potting soil
        Seeds of your favorite herb (best choices for this are chives)
        water
        newspapers

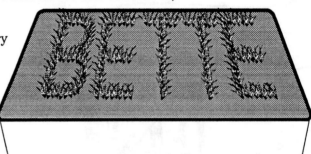

Instead of planting herbs in a flower pot, try sowing the seeds in an aluminum sheet cake pan (approx. 13" x 9" x 2") with several drainage holes punched in bottom. Simply fill the tray with potting soil and then trace your name, i.e. BETTE, with your finger on the surface of the soil (see illustration). Make the letters large, 4" to 6". Now plant your seeds along the traced "Row" you made with your finger. Gently push the seeds into the soil and place in a warm dry spot, a window sill is perfect. Water daily (be sure to place old newspapers under the tray to absorb water running off). Soon tiny sprouts will be peaking up through the soil in the shape of your name. When the herbs are 3" to 5" tall, you're ready to present the whole tray at your next party, so that your guests may help themselves to fresh herbs, in your honor.

Peanut Butter Play Clay

"A DELICIOUSLY EDIBLE MODELING CLAY FOR THOSE WHO BELIEVE THAT A GOOD PIECE OF ARTWORK SHOULD BE EATEN, NOT DISPLAYED."

For this recipe you will need:

        Mixing bowl and spoon
        1/2 cup smooth peanut butter
        1/2 cup of honey
        1 cup dry powdered milk

Mix everything up in a bowl until you have a modeling clay consistency. Add more powdered milk if you need it.

Make sure you play on a clean surface with clean hands. You don't want to eat dirt.

Surprise Christmas Ice Cubes

"COLORFUL, SWEET ICE CUBES ENLIVEN CHRISTMAS PUNCH!"

Freeze green limeade in ice trays with a red maraschino cherry in each tray well. When the ice melts in the glass of punch, a cherry is left behind as an added treat!

Baked Ice Cream Cones
and Frozen Cup Cakes

"AN UNUSUAL TRICKY TREAT THAT LOOKS FROSTY COLD, BUT IS REALLY WARM AND SWEET, OR IS IT THE OTHER WAY AROUND?"

For this recipe you will need:

1 box of wafer type ice cream cones (10-12), make sure they have flat bottoms so they will stand up.

1 box of your favorite cake mix

Eggs, oil and water called for on box of cake mix

Your favorite ice cream and cup cake liners

ICE CREAM   CUP CAKE

Follow the directions on the cake mix box for cupcakes. (Don't forget to preheat the oven) Mix up the batter and fill each cone about 2/3 full. The batter from the box of cake mix should make 12 baked ice cream cones.

Now stand each cone on a cookie sheet and carefully place the sheet in the oven on a center rack. Do this carefully - you don't want any of the filled cones to fall over!

Bake for about 20 minutes, or until the batter puffs up and looks like a big scoop of frosty ice cream sitting on top of the cone.

After the baked ice cream cones are cool, decorate them with your favorite frosting and cake decorating sprinkles. Serve alongside a scoop of real ice cream served in an aluminum cup cake liner decorated to look like a real cupcake, for a real confusing, but tasty dessert.

Self Frosting Cake

"A COMPLETELY FROSTED CAKE READY TO EAT RIGHT OUT OF THE PAN!"

For this recipe you will need:

One 4 oz. bar sweet baking chocolate	1/4 cup sugar
1-1/2 Tablespoon water	1/2 teaspoon salt
1/2 teaspoon vanilla	1/2 cup water
1/2 cup sweetened condensed milk	1/4 cup milk
1-1/3 cups all-purpose flour	4 Tablespoons butter
1 package instant dry yeast	1 egg

Line the bottom of a 9" x 9" x 2" baking pan with two layers of wax paper and lightly grease. Put chocolate broken up into pieces, 1-1/2 Tablespoon water and 1/2 teaspoon vanilla into a double boiler and melt the chocolate. Pour this mixture into the lined baking pan. Set aside.

Combine 1-1/2 cup flour, yeast, 1/4 cup sugar and 1/2 teaspoon salt in a small bowl and mix well. In a separate sauce pan, heat 1/2 cup water, 1/4 cup milk and 2 Tablespoons butter. When mixture is warm (approx. 125 degrees F.), add to the flour mixture. Break the egg into the bowl and blend at low speed until evenly moist. Then beat at medium speed for 3 minutes. Pour this over the chocolate in the baking pan. Melt the remaining 2 Tablespoons butter and brush or drizzle over the top of the batter. Turn oven on to preheat to 375 degrees Now place pan in a warm place for about 4 minutes, or until volume has doubled. Now bake at 375 degrees F. for approx. 25 minutes. Remove from oven and cool about 10 minutes.

While cake is still hot, run knife around edges to loosen and invert onto a large plate. Lift off pan. Wait about 5 minutes before carefully peeling away the waxed paper. Your Self-Frosted cake is ready to eat.

Caramel Cage Covers for Ice Cream

"WEBBED CANDY DOMES FIT OVER A SCOOP OF ICE CREAM AND ARE SHATTERED BEFORE EATING."

For this recipe you will need:
    1/2 cup water
    1 cup sugar
    a pinch of cream of tartar
    aluminum foil
    one 6 oz. ladle
    vegetable oil
    candy thermometer

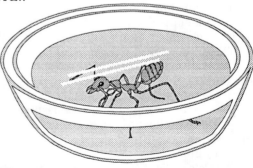

Cover the outside (rounded part) of a 6 ounce ladle with aluminum foil. Making sure to keep the surface smooth and tight. Lightly oil the domed surface of foil.

Now pour into a saucepan the one cup of sugar, 1/2 cup of water and the pinch of cream of tartar. Shake the pan to mix and cover. Heat this covered mixture over medium low heat until the sugar dissolves. Remove the lid and continue cooking the syrup until it turns a light gold color (About 340 degrees F. on your candy thermometer).

Remove the pan from the stove and let it sit at room temperature 6 - 8 minutes. The syrup will turn a darker gold color.

Now you are ready to make the cages. Just hold the foil covered ladle over the pan, dip a spoon into the caramel syrup and drizzle the caramel syrup over the ladle, moving your hand around in a swirling motion to form a web or a lattice pattern on the foil. Prop up the ladle so the caramel cage cools completely (about 10 minutes).

Pry the foil away from the ladle carefully so as not to break the fragile cage. Trim away the uneven strands with scissors to form a nice straight bottom. Now carefully peel off the foil and you have a beautiful candy cage to place over a single scoop of ice cream. Try to find a dish so the cage fits on the edge of the dish. Instruct your guests to tap the cage with the back of a spoon and enjoy the special effect!

Insect in Amber Gelatin Mold

"A VERY POPULAR DINOSAUR MOVIE INSPIRED THIS RECIPE - IT IS GUARANTEED TO BE DINO-MITE!!"

For this recipe you will need:
    1 package peach gelatin
    insect shaped candy
    4 small round or oblong bowls

Follow directions on gelatin package and pour into small bowls. Put in refrigerator for approximately one hour, or until it starts to set up. Remove bowls and suspend candy insects in center of mold and replace in refrigerator. When completely set, dip bowls in warm water to loosen, invert and unmold on plate.

Your guests must drill through their amber mold with their spoon to remove the candy insect first. Then the rest of the treat can be eaten.

Four-Legged Roast Turkey (or Chicken)

"IS IT A NEW SPECIES OF FOWL - OR JUST A FOUL TRICK FOR THAT SUNDAY FAMILY DINNER.

For this recipe you will need:
> 1 whole roasting turkey or chicken (size is your choice)
> 2 extra drumsticks, the same size as your roaster's legs
> sharp carving knife
> poultry needle & thread

Prepare the bird for roasting in your usual manner except for one detail. Take the sharp knife and carefully remove both wings from the bird by pulling the wing away from the breast and slicing through the joint. You want to leave as much skin behind as possible to hide your rigging for the special effect. Save wings and roast separately.

Now take the two separate drumsticks and place them where you removed the wings. Carefully arrange the thick end of the drumstick so it fits into the hole left by the wing. Now take your poultry needle and thread and sew the leg into place onto the wing socket so no thread shows on the outside. Repeat with the other drumstick. You should now have a bird that looks like it has four legs! Don't worry if your rigging is a little sloppy. After the bird is roasted, it will look better.

Now roast as usual and present whole bird at the table while announcing you have prepared a new species of turkey. The drumstick lovers will be pleased and your guests will have a good laugh at your sense of humor.

Bejeweled Anniversary Cake

"A CAKE THAT LOOKS LIKE THE CROWN JEWELS OF ENGLAND?"

For this recipe you will need:
> 2 eight inch cake rounds (purchase or make your favorite)
> white frosting
> Jell-o® Jigglers™ gelatin snacks recipe

Buy Jell-o® and follow Jigglers recipe. While Jell-o® is cooling, frost the cake with white frosting. When Jell-o® Jigglers™ are set, cut into different shaped jewels, i.e.. diamonds, pear shapes, emeralds, etc. Decorate cake with jewels on top and along sides. Keep refrigerated until ready for presentation. "Great for Wedding Anniversaries"

You can also cut Jell-o® shapes that coincide with each different holiday throughout the year....Firecrackers for July 4th, Jack-O-Lanterns for Halloween, Eggs & Bunnies for Easter, etc. The options are unlimited.

Jell-o® is a Registered Trademark of General Foods.

Edible "PLASTIC"

"As tough as the real thing and it looks like stained glass!"

For this recipe you will need:
- 1 envelope Unflavored Gelatin
- 3 Tablespoons water
- Food coloring
- Pie plate

Mix the gelatin, water and food coloring in a saucepan over medium heat. Stir constantly until all the gelatin grains are completely dissolved. Pour the mixture into the pie plate. Let it harden for 48 hours, or until the edges are dry like plastic. The center will still be rubbery.

Cut it into any shape you desire. Make a mobile to hang in a window - it looks just like stained glass - and you can eat it!

Fortune Telling Crystal Ball Gelatine Mold

"Gaze into the crystal and choose your destiny...all in fun!"

For this recipe you will need:
- 4 envelopes unflavored gelatine
- 4 cups colorless (clear) soda-pop (your choice)
- round dome-like mold bowl
- different colors construction paper
- plastic wrap

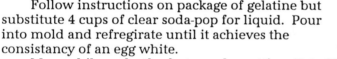

Follow instructions on package of gelatine but substitute 4 cups of clear soda-pop for liquid. Pour into mold and refregirate until it achieves the consistancy of an egg white.

Meanwhile make the fortunes by cutting 4" to 6" strips of differente color paper 1/2" wide. Write different fortunes on each strip. Roll tightly in plastic wrap. Insert fortunes into mold, despersing fortunes throughout. Make sure to have enough for everyone. Let guests spoon their fortune and serving into their own dish.

Braided String Licorice Jewelry

"How to create clever licorice bracelets and necklaces."

Buy lots of red and black string licorice from a candy store. There are also several colors and flavors or rope licorice, which is just a thicker version of the string licorice. Buy several different colors of the ropes too.

Braid 3 different colors together and tie the two ends together. Add candy hearts for charms. Presto: colorful and edible bracelets and necklaces!

Colorful Dinosaur Pizza Face Pizza

"Your kids will REALLY WARM UP TO this lovable dinosaur treat."

For this recipe you will need:

 1 frozen plain cheese pizza
 1 cup shredded mozzarella cheese
 1 small can beets
 black olives
 green olives

Open the can of beets and drain the liquid into a small bowl. Place 1 cup shredded mozzarella cheese into the beet liquid and let stand one minute. Pour off the beet liquid and dry the purple dyed cheese with paper towels. This will not affect the flavor of the cheese. Arrange the purple cheese on the frozen pizza surface to resemble the illustration. Use the olives for the eyes and nostrils. Bake the pizza according to package directions and serve to eager purple dinosaur fans.

Note: You don't need a pizza to do faces. Try arranging the faces right on a plate or pita bread rounds using mashed potatoes, etc.

White Chocolate Baby Dinosaur Egg

"Give birth to a new Easter tradition - a giant white chocolate egg you crack open to reveal a candy Baby Dinosaur inside!"

For this recipe you will need:

 1 plastic sugar egg mold (available at cake decorating store for about $2.00)
 Nonstick cooking spray
 1 pound white "Merckens" (chocolate disks or similar baking chocolate made with paraffin - available at cake decorating store)
 Cotton candy

Melt chocolate over medium heat in double boiler until evenly smooth. Lightly coat each inside egg mold half with nonstick spray. Pour in about 1/2 cup melted chocolate in 1/2 mold and "roll" mold around so gravity makes the chocolate flow over entire inside surface. Pour in more to thicken out any thin spots if necessary. Repeat with other half. Refrigerate 10 - 15 minutes. Save 2 - 3 tablespoons of chocolate to seal egg. Dip each outer egg half in warm water to loosen egg shell and invert it on a plate. Repeat with other half. If you crack or break the shell, remelt and try again.

Place cotton candy nest in bottom half of egg, place candy Dinosaur into cotton candy nest and cover with top half of egg. Seal the seam with remaining melted chocolate, and smooth with your finger.

Your Dinosaur egg is now ready to present. Hatch the egg by rapping the top shell with the back of a spoon to reveal the candy Baby Dinosaur inside!

Edible Fruit Flower Basket

"Now you can give incredible fruit flowers to your love that taste as good as they look."

For this recipe you will need"

    1 small wicker basket available from florist
    1 head of tightly packed leaf lettuce that
       fits snugly into basket
    1 melon baller
    1 package of 8" to 10" bamboo
       skewers (at least 30 skewers)
    assorted colorful fruit like
       strawberries, grapes, blueberries,
       pineapple, cantaloupe, kiwi, etc.

    Place the head of lettuce into the basket making sure it fits snugly into basket so only 1" - 2" of top shows above basket rim. Slice the pineapple into round slices, then cut each round slice into a 6 or 7 pointed star or daisy shape. Cut canteloupe in two and make several melon balls. Stick a skewer through the center of a pineapple flower and put a melon ball on the skewer tip. You have a fruit flower! Place the flower into a bowl of cold water. Make 4 or 5 skewers of 8-9 blueberries and place into cold water. Do the same with strawberries and grapes.

    Now just insert your skewered fruit into the lettuce head, arranging an attractive arrangement just as you would with real flowers. In 5 or 10 minutes you will have a beautiful edible fruit flower bouquet that makes a wonderful gift instead of a boring fruit basket!

Chinese Cabbage Christmas Tree Centerpiece

"Carve a head of Napa into a realistic looking Christmas tree for a holiday table decoration."

For this recipe you will need:
- 1 long, large head of Chinese Napa cabbage (use a large head of regular cabbage if Napa is not available)
- 6" long skewer (bamboo works great)
- red string licorice
- 1 star fruit
- toothpicks

Cut off the foot end of the cabbage so you have a flat bottom on the cabbage so it will stand up. Now push bamboo skewer down through the top of the cabbage as far as it will easily go. Leave about 2" of skewer on top to hold the star. The skewer will hold the leaves together while you carve the tree.

Now slice off the sides of the cabbage in the shape of a tree. (see illustration).

Place several toothpicks into the tree and place the sliced olives onto picks to resemble Christmas bulbs. Drape the red string licorice around the tree to resemble garlands. Cut a slice of star fruit and place it on top of the tree, on the bamboo skewer you left protruding. Rub cabbage with lemon juice if you want to keep it from discoloring. This will keep your tree fresh for a whole week!

Upside Down Pineapple Christmas Tree

" A Hawaiian Holiday table decoration."

For this recipe you will need:
- One pineapple with large undamaged leaves
- Two or three 6" bamboo skewers.
- One grapefruit
- Strawberries or any colored berry or grape
- peanut butter
- powdered sugar
- star fruit

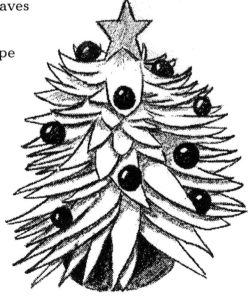

Buy a pineapple with a large growth of leaves. Turn several upside down and judge which one best resembles a Christmas tree. Buy that one. Cut off leaves at top of pineapple, so you have no fruit left at base of leaves. Cut off one slice from the end of the grapefruit so that it stands up. Place two or three 6" bamboo skewers into grapefruit and place upside down leaves into skewers so it stands by itself. Arrange so skewers are not visible. Put toothpick in top and place a slice of star fruit for the top.

Put a dab of peanut butter on each strawberry or other fruit decoration and "glue" it to several leaves. Sprinkle leaves with powdered sugar. Your tree will last for several days.

Recipe Notes:

Section Two
Special Mobile
Effects

Recipe Notes:

How to Make Just About Any Food That Floats Move In Liquid

HOW TO USE EFFERVESCENT TABLETS AS MINIATURE "MOTORS"
TO POWER FLOATING FOOD!

You can make just about any food that floats move through a liquid with effervescent tablets. Just go to your pharmacist and ask for sodium bicarbonate tablets.

When the tablet is attached to a cookie, a small doughnut or any floatable food and placed in a liquid, the fizzing action of the tablet pushes the food object through the liquid. Better still, You can buy effervescent vitamin tablets called "NUTRA FIZZ"™ at any GNC store. ('NUTRA FIZZ is a registered trademark of General Nutrition Corporation). These fizzie vitamin tablets come in several flavors and have 20 vitamins and minerals.

The special effects you can create with effervescent tablets are endless. I have included some of the best on the following pages.

Have fun!

NOTE: If NUTRA FIZZ is not available in your area, substitute with sodium bicarbonate tablets available at your nearest drugstore.

Breakfast Bowl Spinners
(or Mobile Children's Cereal)

"A BREAKFAST CEREAL THAT MOVES AROUND THE BOWL WHEN YOU POUR ON THE MILK"!

For this Special Effect you will need:

- Cookie, wafers, etc.
- Effervescent tablets
- Bowl of milk

Take your most nutritious, low sugar cookie recipe, like peanut butter oatmeal, and bake small cookies in an "S" shape, about two inches long.

Break off small chunks of a sodium bicarbonate tablet and push one chunk into both ends of the "S".

Place the cookie in a bowl of milk and as the bit of effervescent tablet fizzes, the cookie spins around in the bowl of milk. After the fizzing stops, the cookie is eaten and a new one is put in the bowl.

Try putting two or three in at once!

It's even better to use * NUTRA FIZZ™ tablets to power the milk spinners. You get the added benefit of coloring and flavoring the milk (cherry, orange, etc.) along with fortifying the milk with 20 vitamins and minerals.

You can make other shapes too. Try small submarine shapes or jet airplane shapes with a bit of fizz tablet inserted on one end.

NUTRA FIZZ™ is a registered trademark of General Nutrition Corporation, available at GNC stores.

Swimming Cucumber Shark

ADD A NEW "MOBILE DIMENSION" TO YOUR NEXT PUNCH BOWL!

For this Special Effect You will need:

- Small cucumber or zucchini
- Paring knife
- Toothpicks
- Effervescent tablets
- Peanut butter
- Filled punch bowl

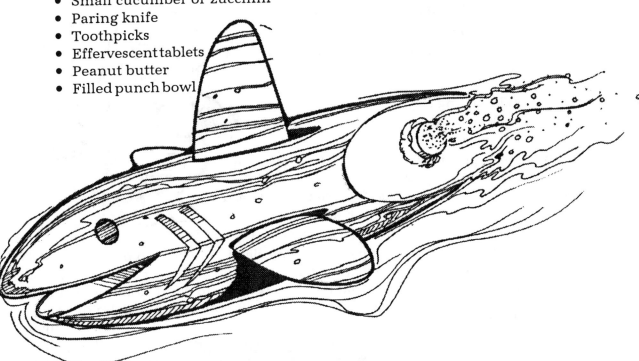

Take a large cucumber and cut a "V" shaped notch into the large end for a mouth. Cut a slash at the corner of the mouth to resemble gills. Hollow out the two eyes. Now cut three slices from the rear end for the fins. Cut out notches for the fins, insert the slices and secure with toothpicks. Now place a dab of peanut butter on the effervescent tablet and place on the rear of the shark . so it sticks.

Now place your shark into a punch bowl and watch as it swims around the bowl. Replace the tablet after it has dissolved.

ALTERNATE TECHNIQUE TO POWER "SWIMMING CUCUMBER SHARK"

To make the Cucumber Shark swim faster, use Alka-Seltzer® tablets instead of just sodium bicarbonate tablets and colored warm water instead of punch. Since these tablets contain aspirin, you don't want to drink the punch - so use warm water colored with food coloring to create the special effect. Don't let anyone drink the water! Pour it down the drain!

Alka-Seltzer® is a registered trademark of MILES, Inc.

Monster in the Popcorn
(Pulsating Popcorn Bowl)

HOW TO MAKE AN ORDINARY BOWL OF POPCORN PULSATE AND SWIRL MYSTERIOUSLY"!
For this Special Effect you will need:

- Plastic wind up toy with large key
- Stiff cardboard
- Glue
- Modeling clay
- Deep bowl
- Popcorn

Buy a cheap plastic wind-up toy. Make sure the toy has a large wind-up key. Now simply glue an "L" shaped armature you cut from a stiff piece of cardboard to the large wind-up key as shown in Fig. 1.

Fig. 1

Place a fist sized lump of modeling clay in the bottom of a deep bowl. Push the adapted "monster mixer" into the clay so that it can be wound up while holding the bowl bottom in the palm of one hand while cranking up the toy with the other hand. The toy will probably have moving feet, so place a cardboard cover over the "monster mixer" so the popcorn won't jam the feet and stop the swirling motion and ruin the special effect. See Fig. 2.

Fig. 2

When ready to serve, crank the toy to the maximum and quickly pour the popcorn into the bowl and watch the children squeal at the popcorn monster swimming under the popcorn. Even Uncle Fester would be proud!

You can give the toy away after the popcorn is eaten as a party favor.

Bubbling Witches Cauldron Soup Bowl

YOUR "MAGIC TOUCH" TURNS ORDINARY SOUP INTO A BUBBLING "SUPER BOWL"!

For this Special Effect you will need:

- Large flat piece of dry ice
- Large Bowl with flat bottom
- Hot soup/stew

BUBBLE, BUBBLE TOIL & TROUBLE! Make a super bubbling witches brew that will astonish your guests at the dinner table. They'll ask, "How do you make it bubble like that?"

Your secret is that you're really cooling the hot soup/stew, not heating it up!

Place a 2" square of dry ice with one flat side, flat side down in a soup tureen or bowl with a flat bottom and let stand about

30-45 seconds. The dry ice will freeze to the bottom of the bowl and stick so when you gently pour the hot soup or stew into the bowl it will bubble like crazy!

The effect will last for several minutes until the CO_2 has evaporated and helped cool your soup too.

Cookie Car that Actually Runs

"KIDS, NOT TIRES WILL SQUEAL WITH DELIGHT AS THIS COOKIE CAR RUNS "IN THE MONEY"!

For this Special Effect you will need:

- Two large cookies, 3" to 4" across
- Three candy canes about 5" long
- Large rubber band about 10" long when cut
- Lead fishing sinker or bolt with loop taped to it

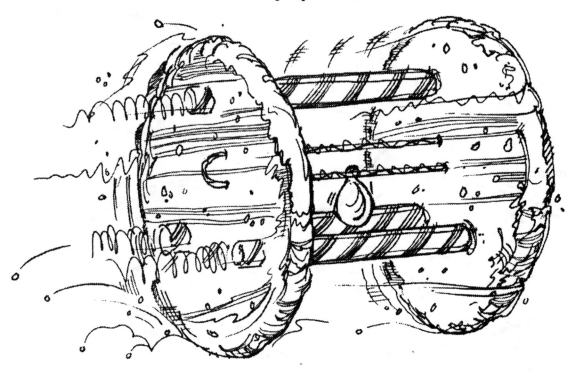

Boys love this. They can make several and have races. The winner gets to keep the cookie car he beats. Or, you can use two cookies of slightly different sizes, so the cookie car runs in circles.

Now push the candy canes into the cookies as shown to form the wheel base. Poke two holes in each cookie about two inches apart and thread the cut rubber band through as shown. Thread the lead sinker onto the rubber band and tie the rubber band together so it is holding the sinker off the ground.

Now roll the cookie car slowly in the opposite direction you want it to run.

Dancing Raisins

HOW TO JAZZ UP DULL SODA POP"

For this Special Effect you will need:

- Several fresh, soft raisins
- Carbonated beverage
- Bicarbonate of soda (optional)

Add three or four raisins to a freshly poured glass of ginger ale or any clear carbonated beverage and watch the raisins rise as they collect bubbles and fall as they give up their bubbles at the surface.

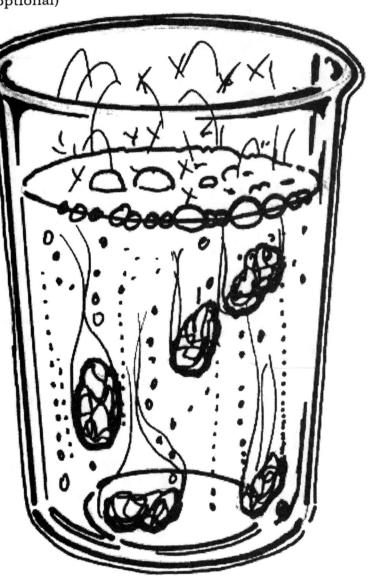

You can speed up the action of the raisins by adding a little bicarbonate of soda. Better still, add a *"NUTRA FIZZ"™ tablet to the drink for added activity and a nutritional kick to the empty calories of the soda POP.

NOTE: If NUTRA FIZZ is not available in your area, substitute with sodium bicarbonate tablets available at your nearest drugstore.

"NUTRA FIZZ"™ is a registered trademark of General Nutrition Corporation, available at GNC stores.

The Great Earthquake Cake

"A CAKE THAT ACTUALLY SHAKES AND QUAKES THEN SPLITS IN TWO BEFORE YOUR STARTLED EYES".

For this recipe you will need:
- One 13" x 9" sheet cake (buy or make your favorite)
- Frosting of your Choice
- Cardboard base for cake, same size as cake or slightly larger.
- Two or three foot length of plastic tube (available at hardware store)
- One regular size balloon (10" - 12" round)
- One can pressurized Whipped Cream

Buy a can of pressurized whipped cream and take it to a hardware store. Buy 2 feet of plastic hose that will fit snugly onto the plastic nozzle of the whipped cream can. If you can't find a hose that fits tightly, come as close as you can. You can build up the width of the nozzle of the can by wrapping tape around the nozzle until the hose fits.

Now take the cardboard base of the cake and cut it into two equal pieces lengthwise. Take can of whipped cream and holding upside down, empty about half of the contents into a bowl for additional frosting. Now take balloon and fasten securely on one end of the hose, taping or tying so that no air can escape. Lay the balloon and hose on table where you want to display the cake. Other end of hose should be over the edge of the table, attached to the top of the whipped cream can nozzle, sitting on a chair. Place cardboard base on table over balloon so that each half of the cardboard rests on top of balloon with hose under a full piece of board. Next, place whole sheet cake on cut cardboard base so cut line is in center of cake. Now make a jagged cut across center of cake, cutting it into two pieces along the cut line of the cardboard base.

Frost the cake and decorate it with small plastic Monopoly buildings, trees, etc. Make it look like a city-scape. You are now ready for the special effect. Sit in the chair and hold the whipped cream can in one hand in an upright position. Hold the hose firmly on the nozzle with the other hand. Announce that you think you feel an earthquake and depress the nozzle for one or 2 seconds, two or three times. This will partially inflate the balloon enough to make the cake slightly rise up. Then depress nozzle again for 3 to 5 seconds and the balloon will push up the center of the cake, revealing the jagged edges and pulling & stretching the frosting across the gap. Pull the hose away from the nozzle slightly and the cake slowly sinks back into position. Repeat as long as your pressurized can lasts. Most folks want to see this several times, so have fun!

Spitting Eggplant Dinosaur with Chomping Jaws

"MOVABLE JURASSIC JAWS AND A SPECIAL SPITTING EFFECT RECREATES THE FUN OF THE MOVIES IN THIS TRENDY TABLE DECORATION".

For this recipe you will need:
- 1 medium sized eggplant
- 1 small yellow summer squash or zucchini
- 1 large pineapple
- 1 small carrot
- 4 medium whole pickles
- 30 almonds

Optional spitting effect ingredients:
- 1 can cola
- 1 two foot length of plastic tube or hose from hardware store
- 1 large meat syringe or plastic squeeze bottle
- tape
- 1 large leaf of red tipped leaf lettuce
- toothpicks

First cut and assemble dinosaur.. Take the pineapple and cut off the leaves. Lay pineapple on its side and slice 1/2" off the rear section, so pineapple can stand up straight. Cut the yellow summer squash in two pieces. One half is the neck. Discard the other half. Carve out a hole in the top of the pineapple slightly smaller than the diameter of the squash. Fit squash neck in hole. Cut off 1/2" from ends of 4 pickles and stand up alongside pineapple for the legs. Cut small hole in back of pineapple and insert carrot for the tail. Now carve the head from the eggplant. Carve out the jaws about 4" to 5" deep from the narrow end of the eggplant. Make sure the jaws are about 2" apart. Carve out eyes and nostrils. Now stick the almonds into the carved jaws for the teeth. Stagger them for a jagged effect. Now carve out a hole at the other end and fit it onto the squash neck. You can manually squeeze the jaws together and they will automatically spring back, due to the rubbery texture of the eggplant. Use toothpicks to secure the parts if necessary.

Optional spitting effect:

Poke a hole through the back of the mouth in the eggplant head (where the throat would be) the same size as your plastic hose, about 1/4" in diameter. Insert your hose from the rear of the head until it begins to aprear in the dinosaur's mouth. The other end of the hose should be behind and under the table. Put a placemat, doily or other cover over hose leading from pineapple if necessary. Fill the meat syringe with cola, insert tip into hose and tape securely. Transform the dinosaur into a spitting dinosaur by placing the leaf lettuce in a fan like pattern around the head and secure it with toothpicks. Cut a slice from a pickle and then slice pickle slice into two half circles. Use these as the crests on top of the Dinosaurs head. Just cut two slits into eggplant and insert flat end of pickle (see illustration). When ready to demonstrate the spitting effect, hold the syringe under the table and give a warning about spitting dinosaurs, then squeeze out short bursts of cola at unsuspecting guests! Challenge them to catch it in their mouths and win a prize! (Have cleanup kit available.)

T-Rex Popcorn Ball Centerpiece

"A GIANT CANDIED POPCORN DINOSAUR WITH A BOBBING HEAD"

For this recipe you will need:

 6 quarts of popped corn
 2 cups of sugar
 2/3 cup light corn syrup
 2/3 cup of water
 1/2 cup margarine
 2 teaspoons salt
 1-1/2 teaspoons vanilla extract
 1 small bottle green food coloring
 1 very large mixing pan
 peanut butter
 candy corn
 1/2" thick x 8" heavy spring from
  hardware store.
 Rubber gloves

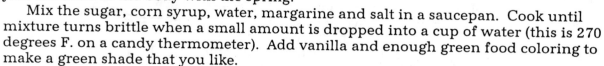

Cover the table with wax paper. You will need a large work surface. Plan ahead so you know exactly how you are going to mold and sculpt the body and head separately. When the 2 popcorn dinosaur parts cool, you can join the head to the body with the spring.

Mix the sugar, corn syrup, water, margarine and salt in a saucepan. Cook until mixture turns brittle when a small amount is dropped into a cup of water (this is 270 degrees F. on a candy thermometer). Add vanilla and enough green food coloring to make a green shade that you like.

Pour 1-1/2 to 2 quarts of popped corn into the very large mixing bowl and slowly pour candy mixture over popcorn. Quickly mix with your greased hands (wear rubber gloves). Transfer mixture to wax paper and form the head shape with wide open jaws.

Do the same for the body, but work in small batches, gradually forming the body with the remaining popcorn.

Let both parts cool. Decorate them by gently pushing wide end of candy corn into jaws for teeth. Use peanut butter for glue if necessary. Glue on 2 red cinnamon disks for eyes. You can decorate the body with scales by using colored frosting in a tube with a small tip. Drill a hole in the bottom of the head and top of the body, slightly smaller than the spring. Insert the spring into the body and place the head on top of the spring. You now have a fun and tasty centerpiece with a bobbing head for your party table.

Snake Charmer's Cake

"DO YOU DARE TAKE THE LID OFF THE BASKET AND PLAY THE COBRA SONG ON YOUR FLUTE...BEWARE?"

For this recipe you will need:

One angle food cake

Frosting in a tube with decorating tips

1 large cookie that fits top of cake as lid

2 foot length of 3/8" to 1/2" plastic hose

1 can pressurized whipped cream

large sheets of tissue wrapping paper

masking tape

card table

waxed paper

toy flutes or kazoo

Place waxed paper on top of card table and position cake on paper near one side of table about 6-8" from the edge of table. Put the hose up the center hole of the cake about 2 inches from the top. The cake should have a 1/2" groove cut in the bottom to accommodate the hose. Tape the hose to the table so that it will not move. You should have 12" of hose hanging off the edge of the table. Frost the cake any color you like. Then with the decorating tube and tip with the small round hole, make a lattice pattern on the frosting to resemble a wicker basket. Do the same with the cookie cover. Crinkle up the tissue and arrange it around the cake to hide the tube and make a pretty surrounding for the cake. Sit in a chair and insert the nozzle of whipped cream can into the hose. Build up diameter of the nozzle with tape if necessary so that the tube fits snugly. Hold the tube tightly with one hand and the whipped cream can with the other. (When ready for the special effect, be sure to turn can upside down.) Give everyone a toy flute or kazoo and instruct them to play a cobra song. Take off the cover from the cake and lean it up against the cake. When your guests have played a few bars of a tune, depress the nozzle quickly so the whipped cream pipes it's way through the hose and up through the top of the basket. The "Snake" of whipped cream will climb straight up 8 to 12 inches over the basket before falling over! Repeat if desired....it will be desired!

Three Foot Worm Cheese Sandwich

"SQUEEZE OUT A THREE FOOT CHEESE WORM TRAPPED INSIDE A POCKET BREAD - DON'T WORRY - IT TASTES GREAT AND LOOKS GREAT TOO - IF YOU GET PAST THE IDEA!"

For this recipe you will need:

Several pita pocket bread rounds (preferably day old, the bread should be slightly dry and stiff)

1 can cheese product in pressurized can

Take one round of pocket bread and carefully cut a small 1/4" hole in the center - but only through the top layer of bread - don't cut through both layers.

Next place a chopstick, pencil or some other small stick into hole and pry open the two layers of bread. Do this all the way around to loosen any stuck parts to make the pocket inside as wide open as possible. Be careful not to tear the layers apart!

Once you have opened the insides sufficiently - take the can of pressurized cheese and insert nozzle into hole in pocket bread. Push nozzle all the way sideways and depress nozzle gently - filling pocket with cheese from the edges to the center. It's important to pump cheese into edges first and then work toward the center hole. Pump up the bread as much as you can with the cheese.

Now take the sandwich in both hands and gently squeeze from edge to center. The 3 foot cheese worm trapped inside will squish out to be devoured by a hungry kid-bird.

Section Three
Special Sound
Effects

Recipe Notes:

Singing Cake

"GATHER YOUR FRIENDS AROUND THIS BAKING CAKE AND WHISTLE A MERRY TUNE ALONG WITH THE CAKE"!

This is the only recipe in the whole book where you have to use the ingredients listed to make the actual cake. The whole effect depends on these ingredients, so try not to change a thing!

You will need:

- 1 cup butter
- 2 cups brown sugar
- 2 tsp. baking powder mixed in 1 cup of buttermilk
- 1 cup raisins
- 2 tsp. cinnamon
- 2 sq. bitter chocolate melted
- 3 eggs separated
- 1 cup strawberry jam
- 1 cup chopped nuts
- 1 tsp. cloves
- 4 cups sifted flour

Cream butter and sugar. Add egg yolks and stir. Add melted chocolate and stir. Add raisins and stir. Add cinnamon, cloves, flour and stir. Add nuts and jam and stir.

Now add the baking powder to the buttermilk and quickly add to the cake mixture and stir. Fold in the stiffly beaten egg whites. Quickly pour mix into greased and floured angel food cake pan . Bake at 350 degrees F. until cake stops singing, about 45 minutes.

Make sure you time this recipe so your quests are present during the baking. Once the cake is baked the effect is over.

Talking Soda Pop
(Juice., Water., Any Liquid)

HOW TO TURN DULL, UNINTERESTING DRINKS INTO A FUN, SOUND EFFECTS PARTY"!

For this Special Effect you will need:

- "POP ROCKS"™ Action Candy*
- Juice, water, soda pop, etc.

The secret to this special effect is in a special "Action Candy" called *"POP ROCKS"™. This candy is processed with carbon dioxide which is released as a crackling, popping sound when it comes in contact with water.

To create the special effect, simply drop a few "rocks" into a glass of soda pop, punch or any liquid and it will immediately pop loudly, then sink to the bottom and then crackle until the rock is completely dissolved. This takes several minutes, then you can add more candy, if your guests have not already finished their noisy drinks.

* If "POP ROCKS"" are not available in your area, "FIZZ-WIZ" popping candy or "CRAZY DIPS" crackling candy may be substituted.

*"POP ROCKS"" is a registered trademark of General Foods Corporation.

Crackling Cupcakes

"TRANSFORM ORDINARY CAKE INTO A TOTAL MOUTH ENTERTAINING EXPERIENCE"!

For this Special Effect you will need:

- "POP ROCKS"™ Action Candy*
- Cupcakes, Sliced cake, etc.

Simply push several rocks of *"POP ROCKS"™ candy into cupcakes, cookies, cake slices or any treat your kids love.

When eaten, the candy reacts with the saliva in the mouth creating a crackling and popping sensation on the tongue and in the mouth, a sensation children love.

* If "POP ROCKS"" are not available in your area, "FIZZ-WIZ" popping candy or "CRAZY DIPS" crackling candy may be substituted.

*"POP ROCKS"™ is a registered trademark of General Foods Corporation.

Recipe Notes: